The Heart of a River

By Eileen Delehanty Pearkes

Illustrations by Nichola Lytle

RMB

For information on purchasing bulk quantities of this book, or to obtain media excerpts or invite the author to speak at an event, please visit rmbooks.com and select the "Contact" tab.

RMB | Rocky Mountain Books Ltd.
rmbooks.com
@rmbooks
facebook.com/rmbooks

Cataloguing data available from Library and Archives Canada
ISBN 9781771606998 (hardcover)
ISBN 9781771607001 (softcover)
ISBN 9781771607018 (electronic)

Printed and bound in China

We would like to also take this opportunity to acknowledge the traditional territories upon which we live and work. In Calgary, Alberta, we acknowledge the Niitsítapi (Blackfoot) and the people of the Treaty 7 region in Southern Alberta, which includes the Siksika, the Piikuni, the Kainai, the Tsuut'ina, and the Stoney Nakoda First Nations, including Chiniki, Bearpaw, and Wesley First Nations. The City of Calgary is also home to Métis Nation of Alberta, Region III. In Victoria, British Columbia, we acknowledge the traditional territories of the Lkwungen (Esquimalt and Songhees), Malahat, Pacheedaht, Scia'new, T'Sou-ke, and W̱SÁNEĆ (Pauquachin, Tsartlip, Tsawout, Tseycum) peoples.

We acknowledge the financial support of the Government of Canada through the Canada Book Fund and the Canada Council for the Arts, and of the province of British Columbia through the British Columbia Arts Council and the Book Publishing Tax Credit.

I would like you all to imagine for a moment

that you are water.

Not water in a glass,

still and calm as a lake,

but water being poured,

water on a journey,

water moving downhill

to the sea.

Imagine yourself tangled by rocks

and narrowed by canyons.

Imagine yourself humbled to the land.

That has always been my experience.

I am the Columbia River.

This is my story:

The earliest memories I have of myself are very faint.

Like your earliest childhood memories,

I cannot remember much about when

I first came into being.

I know I have flowed for close to 20 million years.
I know I changed course many times
as volcanoes erupted and lava bubbled
across the Pacific Northwest.
Then ice completely covered the land
I journeyed across.

I continued to flow, but more slowly

and with greater depth as I carved a path

through and under glaciers.

When the ice began to melt, it shifted and shaped,

helping to sculpt this mountain terrain.

After most of the glaciers had disappeared,

I settled into a path through the valleys

I still follow today.

You are all old enough to know:
nothing that becomes big and grand
starts out that way.

It is the same with a river.

I begin my journey across the land as a trickle –
in a wetland in the Rocky Mountain Trench.
I flow north for a while, growing larger and stronger
and more defined, before I bend south
through the Purcell and Selkirk mountains
toward the sea.

It has always been my goal to reach the ocean.

All water wishes to join its great mother,

the expanse of salt sea

where many fish swim free.

For thousands of years, I worked freely,

but with care and diligence,

throughout the four seasons.

As the air warmed in spring,

I began to receive melting snow from the land.

By early summer, I would swell like the belly of a whale

as I passed through the mountains.

I would foam and swirl, pausing occasionally in lakes,

racing splendidly through canyons and over falls.

When my water rose each year,

it moistened many wetlands where reed grasses swayed,

songbirds danced high in the cottonwood trees,

and ducks floated on the pulsing stillness.

Some years,

when the snow melted quickly and there was a great deal of it,

I grew overwhelmed with my task.

I swelled up and over my banks, flooding beyond the wetlands,

filling the narrow valleys to the brim.

When these great floods happened, fish swam among berry bushes.

Trees seemed to grow from my water.

In midsummer and into the autumn,

just like an ocean breath being inhaled,

I brought salmon back from the coast.

Down at the place where my waters greeted the sea,

the coho and sockeye and Chinook climbed onto the back of my current.

They needed cool mountain streams to spawn the next generation.

They moved up in my waters to the birthplace we shared,
the Columbia Mountains.

I like to think that each year

I brought a memory of the sea

back into the mountains...

when I carried the salmon home.

I like to think I threaded together
the ancient beads of water and land,
salmon and bear,
fisher and food.

In winter I grew still.

In places I froze hard.

Fish moved into my deepest waters,

underneath the ice.

This was my time of rest
and deep dreaming.

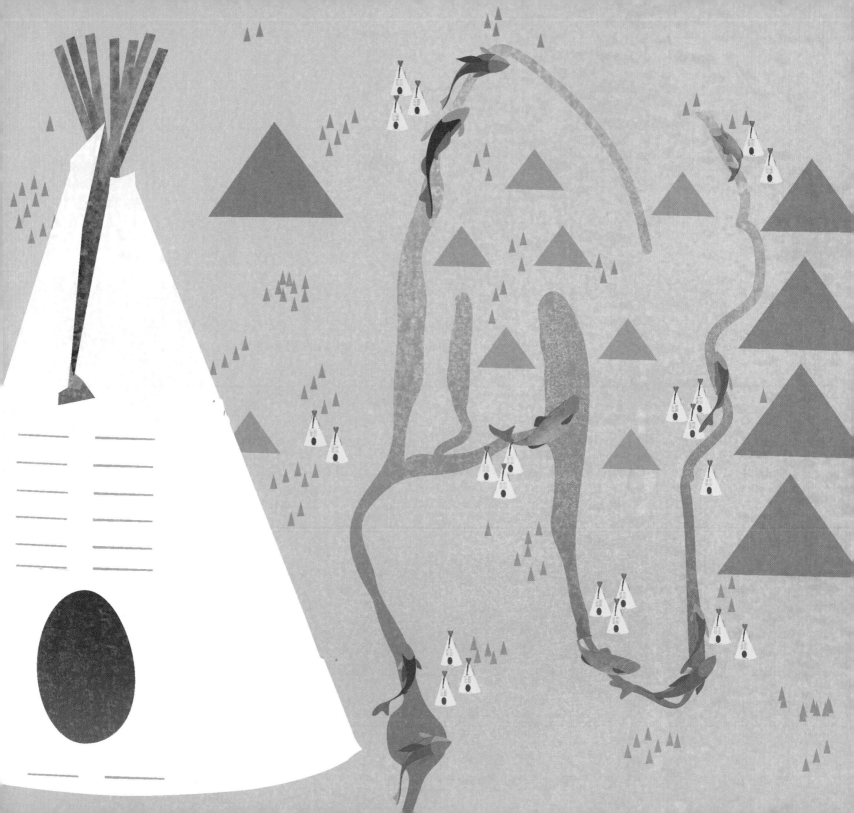

Five thousand years ago,

or even longer,

I began to share my riches with people.

The Sn̓ʕaýckstx (Sinixt) followed the salmon upstream,

moving further and further into the Columbia Mountains,

establishing villages at every turn of my flow.

For a great long time,

the Sinixt lived the life of river people.

They fished for the salmon I carried

on the back of my current.

They dipped their tightly woven baskets

into the clean water at my edges.

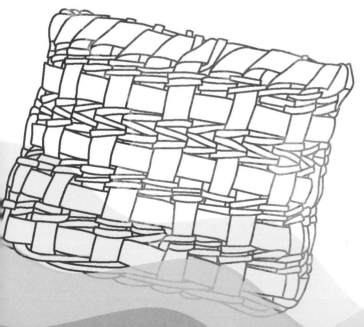

They stroked the stillness of the Arrow Lakes
with their carefully carved paddles
and maneuvered their sturgeon-nosed canoes
through my currents.

They lived by my flowing rhythms.

They buried their dead on my banks.

About 200 years ago, some men

pale as river stones

came across the Rocky Mountains from the northeast.

They were ragged and tired, and I could feel their dislike

of my rocky turbulence.

I know they found my waters cold and unfriendly.

They wanted to share my path to the ocean.

They travelled with effort, in canoes turned up at the ends,

a design unsuited to my rough waters.

They struggled.

I could see that.

But I was not able to change how I had flowed for so long,

just to increase the ease of their passage.

I continued to do what I had always done:

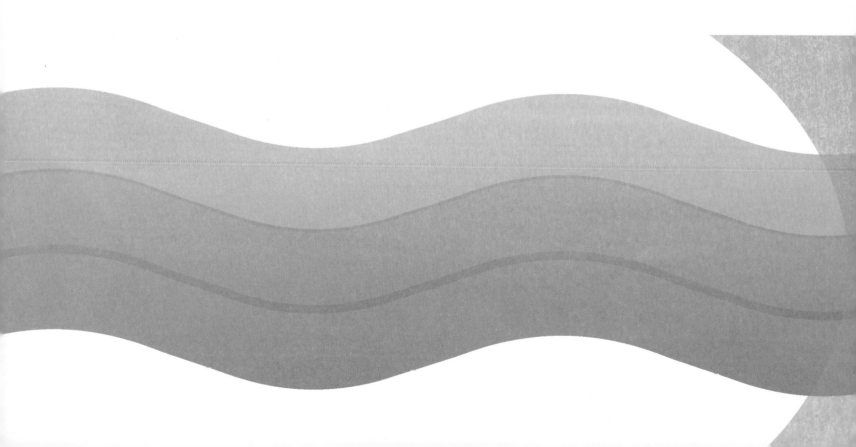

to find my way with great freedom and power to the sea.

These men did not seem interested in the salmon.

They wanted furs, not the river food.

They built houses from trees set close together,

with all the green trimmed away.

There on my banks,

they lit fires and invited the First People in

to trade hides from the beaver, the muskrat, the otter, and the bear.

They taught the Sinixt a trade language called Chinook Jargon.

After that,

when the Sinixt carried the boats of these fur men in portage,

they pointed to the waterfalls and rapids and said *tum tum.*

This was their Chinook Jargon word for the human heart,

but also for my free spirit, for my river will.

Tum wata.

Water with a heart.

About that time, I noticed

some of the Sinixt villages becoming still.

Over the roar of my own water, I heard

the moan of sick and dying people.

I felt them plunge into me to cool their fevers,

and I noticed more and more burials taking place on the shore.

I knew something was wrong in the land,

but I continued to flow along past the emptying villages.

I hoped these people,

who had so long lived beside my banks,

would regain their health and prosperity.

Larger boats came, carrying black-clothed men
and some women – all pale as a white river stone.
They stopped in the same places where the fur men had built their homes
from trees trimmed bare.

They carried small black books

and gathered the Sinixt around to speak to them

with arms extended

and palms turned toward the sky.

I continued to flow in my own way.

I meant these river travellers no harm.

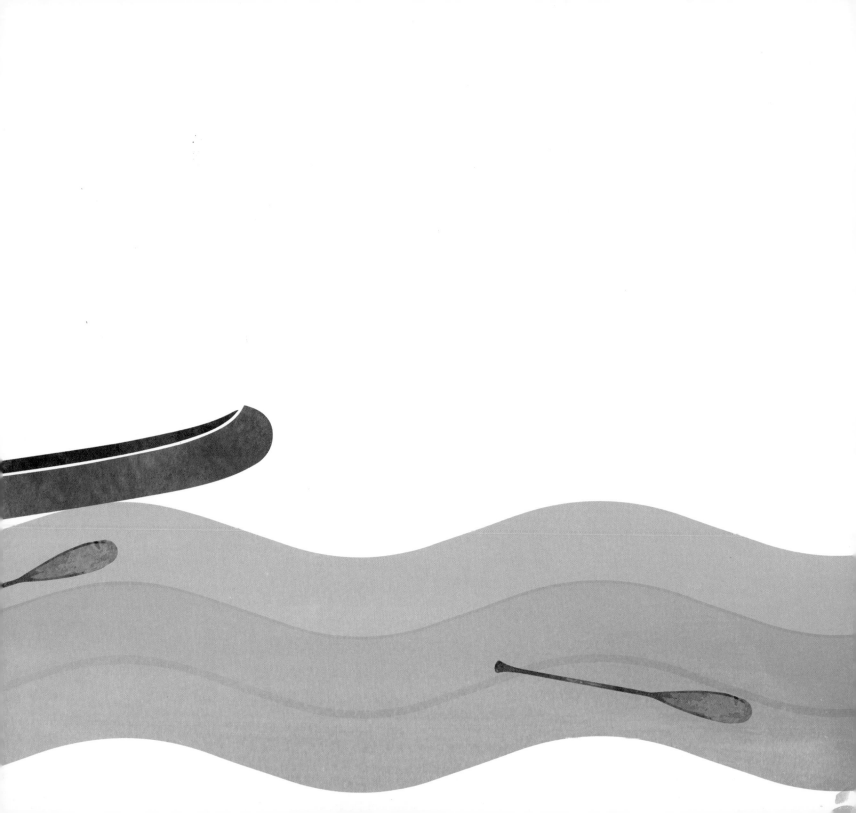

Once, a boat filled with them lost its balance in my current.

The canoe turned over quickly, and I am sorry to say

that, in my rush to the sea,

I swept some of them away with me.

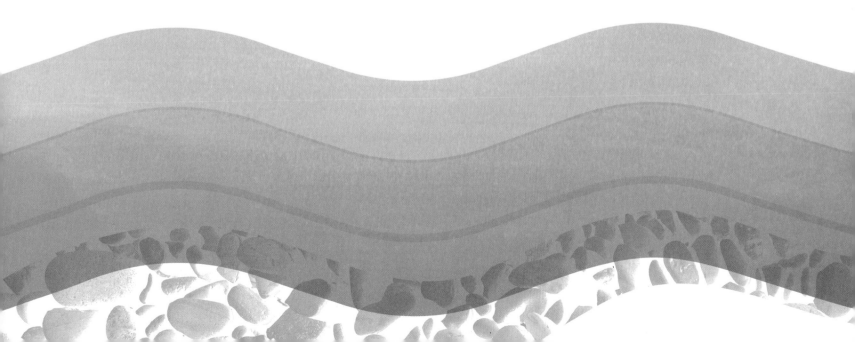

A few decades later, I began to feel the weight
of large, flat-bottomed boats on my water,
river steamers carrying people and supplies
to new, smooth-sided buildings
along my banks.

Above me,

in the bow of a flat-bottomed boat,

I saw a Sinixt man guiding the captain

along the swirling current.

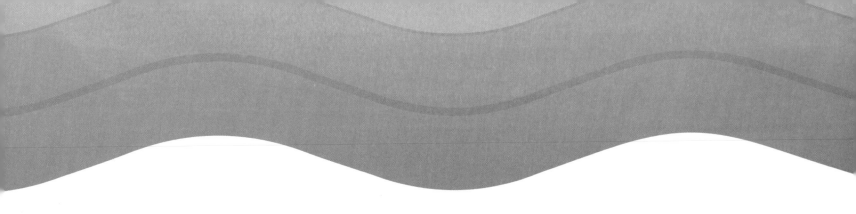

I rarely saw any other Sinixt People
fishing along my banks anymore.
They were no longer busy
with basket traps and harpoons.

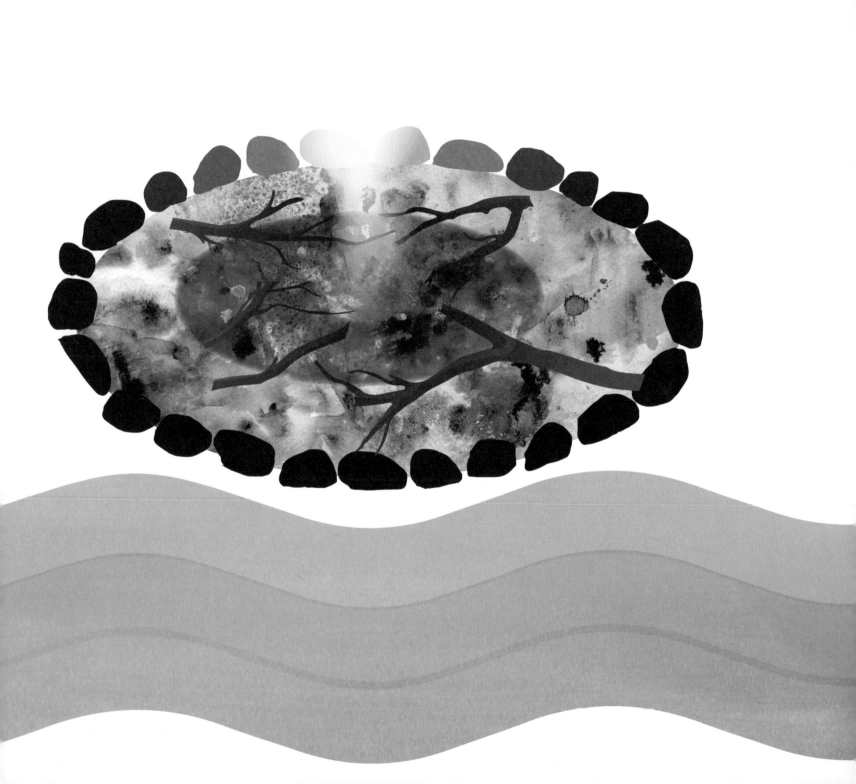

Their villages had been dismantled,

or buried by towns.

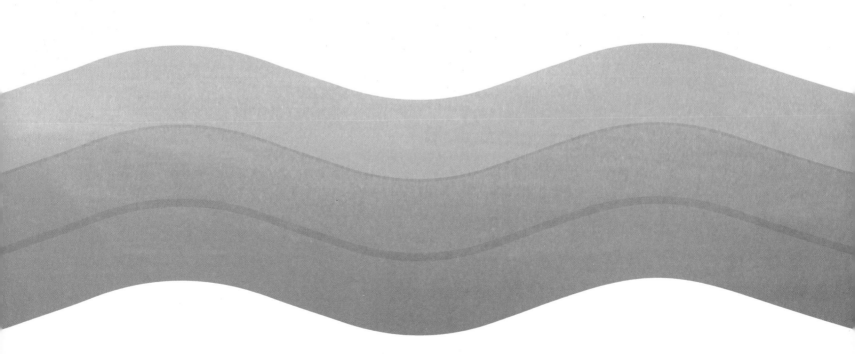

I saw fires sweeping the valleys and hillsides.

I saw miners searching the creeks for gold.

I continued to flow through all these changes.

A few times,

as usual,

I became overwhelmed by my task.

My waters reached very high,

flooding the narrow valleys, the bustling towns,

the farmlands, and orchards marked out

by some of the passengers travelling

in the flat-bottomed boats.

The people

pale as river stones

had built their cities and towns

right near the water's edge.

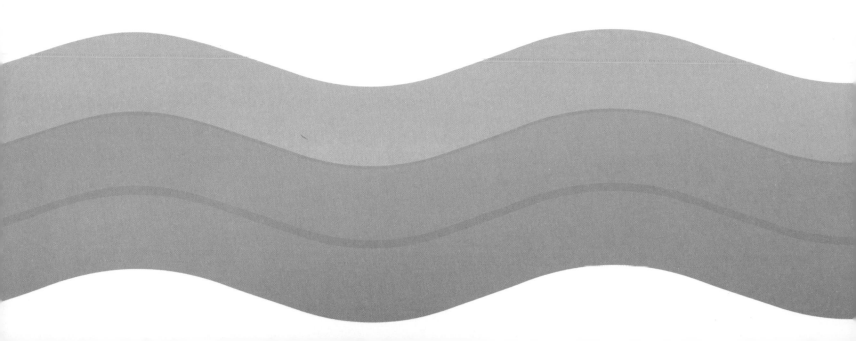

What could I do when the snow was very deep
and the melt so sudden?

I had no choice.

My work was, as it always had been,

to carry the water to the sea.

To empty the mountains of their melting, white burden and

bring back the salmon.

To moisten the many wetlands lining my banks.

There is not much more to tell.

Only 150 years after the people

pale as river stones

arrived, they devised a way to take

my river heart for their own uses,

to change how I had flowed for millions of years.

The concrete gates they built from bank to bank

kept me from bringing the salmon back.

They said they needed to capture

my energy as it fell to the sea.

They said it was being wasted.

They said dams would not harm me,

or the landscape I flowed across.

I could not imagine why they would do such a thing to me.

I wondered if they had grown angry about my waters swelling so high, something I could do nothing about.
I wondered if they harboured ill feelings for the few deaths I caused in the place they called Les Dalles des Morts, the rocky rapids of the dead.

I must admit I am nearly dead myself.

Now

I am a river whose heart

struggles to pulse

with the rhythms of life.

I am a river whose work has been interrupted

by a prosperity I do not recognize,

whose spirit is impoverished and silenced.

I wonder how the people

pale as river stones

could understand so little about my purpose,

what I was born for:

to find my way with great freedom and power

to the sea.

But I am still hopeful.

Someday

I will again be able

to carry the salmon

on the back of my currents.

My *tum wata* will beat hard and strong

as I move through the mountains

to greet the sea.

I will be able to share
my spirit with the land
and its people.

For I am the giver of life

and freedom.

I am water,

the heart of a landscape.

I am the Columbia River.

Columbia River Basin

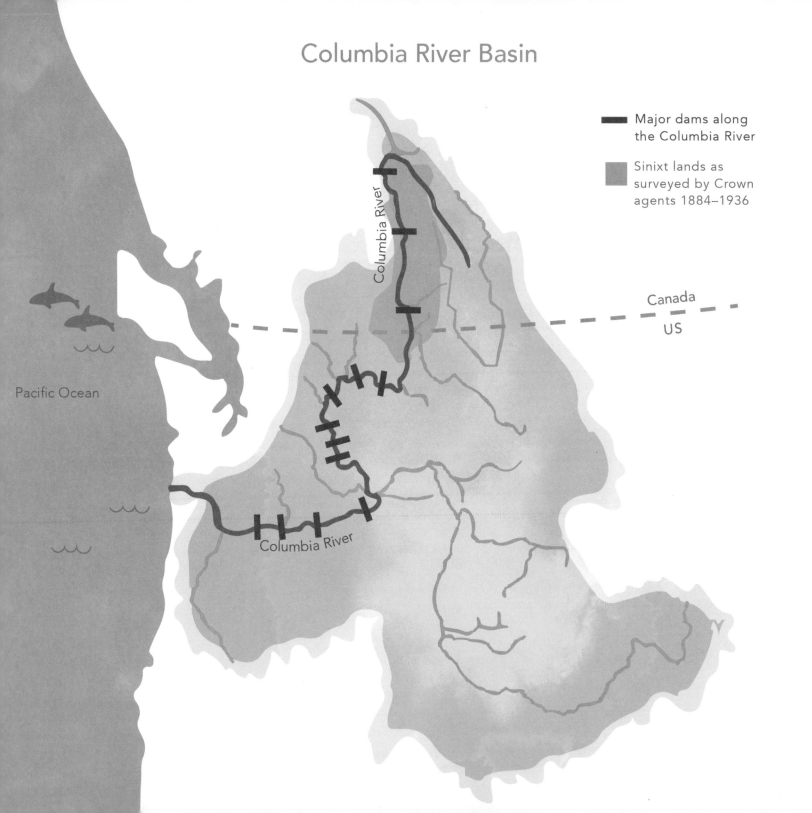

Major dams along the Columbia River

Sinixt lands as surveyed by Crown agents 1884–1936

Canada

US

Pacific Ocean

Columbia River

Columbia River

More about the Columbia

The Columbia River watershed is the fourth-largest by volume in North America, and the largest to empty into the Pacific. Flowing 2000 kilometres (1,250 miles), the river drains an international basin including portions of seven US states (Washington, Oregon, Idaho, Montana, Wyoming, Utah, and Nevada) and one Canadian province (British Columbia). Nearly two dozen modern tribal organizations in both countries claim portions of the great river basin as traditional homeland.

The Columbia River is a snow-charged system that depends on winter precipitation for its flow. It reaches natural flood stage in late spring.

The three ocean salmon native to the Columbia are Chinook (king), coho, and sockeye. Steelhead, an ocean trout, also spawns in the basin. These four species were extirpated from the Upper Columbia region (defined as upstream of Kettle Falls, Washington, to the headwaters in the Rocky Mountain Trench) when the US government completed the Grand Coulee Dam in central Washington in 1941-1942. In August 2019, the Colville Confederated Tribes released the first Chinook above Grand Coulee Dam in 80 years. Some of these fish spawned. While they could not migrate to the ocean, they grew to adulthood in fresh water, and some were caught by fishers a few years later in the reservoir system above the international boundary.

In the Nation's Interior Salish dialect, Sinixt means "People from the Bull Trout Place." Their territory stretches from Kettle Falls, Washington, north to Revelstoke, BC, along the main stem of the Upper Columbia and its tributaries. The Canadian government declared the Sinixt "extinct" in 1956. They continue to exist and have rights in the United States. Between 2017 and 2019, three levels of BC courts confirmed Sinixt Aboriginal Rights under section 35 of the Canadian Constitution in *R. v. Desautel*.

Several tribes in the Upper Columbia watershed have used their own versions of the sturgeon-nosed canoe, including the Ya qannu ki (Ktunaxa) and the Kalispel.

The first recorded fur trader in the Upper Columbia region was cartographer and explorer David Thompson, arriving in 1807. Chinook Jargon (Chinuk Wawa) was a hybrid of various Salish languages that integrated French and English words after colonial settlement. It was widely spoken throughout the Columbia Basin in the 19th century.

European diseases (measles, diphtheria, and smallpox) reduced Columbia Basin Indigenous populations by as much as 80 per cent. Best estimates are that the first waves of disease arrived in the Upper Columbia River region in the 1780s, with successive waves of illness and loss for nearly a century.

On October 22, 1838, a party of Hudson's Bay Company fur traders, botanists, and their families upturned their heavily loaded boat in rough water a short distance below Death Rapids. In all, 12 people died, including five children, the youngest of whom was 24 days old.

In the mid-1860s, the first steam-powered boat on the Columbia transported miners from Marcus, Washington, to the gold fields north of Revelstoke, BC. By the turn of the century, steamers were common throughout the region, connecting railways and otherwise inaccessible communities.

The use of dams for hydro power dates back to the 1890s in the Upper Columbia region. In the 20 years following ratification of the Columbia River Treaty (1964), six major dams dramatically altered the ecology of the upper river basin: Duncan, Mica, Libby, Hugh Keenleyside, Seven Mile, and Revelstoke.

Dive Further

Readers of all ages and educators alike can dive further into the growing body of literature related to the Columbia River. It's a rich history of Indigenous culture from headwaters to mouth, of the fur trade and its impacts, and the many hydro-electric and flood-control dams that mark its watershed today.

A River Captured: The Columbia River Treaty and Catastrophic Change, by Eileen Delehanty Pearkes (Rocky Mountain Books, 2024). A detailed account of how and why the upper Columbia River region became the most heavily dammed ecosystem in the west.

The Geography of Memory: Reclaiming the Cultural, Natural, and Spiritual History of the Snayackstx (Sinixt) First People, by Eileen Delehanty Pearkes (Rocky Mountain Books, 2022). An authorized history of the Sinixt People of the Columbia River headwater mountains.

The Columbia River, by John A. Harrison (Arcadia Publishing, 2021). An exploration of the river's natural and human histories, through photographs taken prior to and after the dams.

Salmon: A Fish, the Earth and the History of Their Common Fate, by Mark Kurlansky (Patagonia, 2020). An overview of the genus and its many species, the biology of its transformation, and its tragic struggle to survive on the Columbia.

Beholden: A Poem as Long as the River, by Rita Wong and Fred Wah (Talonbooks, 2018). Written by two BC poets, the verse follows the shape of the river's geography.

Chinook Resilience: Heritage and Cultural Revitalization on the Lower Columbia River, by Jon D. Daehnke (University of Washington Press, 2017). A collaborative ethnography of how the Chinook Nation continues to move forward and remain resilient, despite their land and heritage being under assault.

A River Lost, by Lynn Bragg and Virgil Smoker Marchand (Strong Nations Publishing, 2009). A story for all ages in which Sinee mat and her great-grandmother Toopa tell how the Grand Coulee Dam destroyed the way of life of the Arrow Lakes People.

B Street: The Notorious Playground of Coulee Dam, by Lawney L. Reyes (University of Washington Press, 2008). Named after the street where dam workers spent their wages and blew off steam, a personal account of how the building of the Grand Coulee Dam forever changed the lives of one Indigenous family and devastated the Sin-Aikst (Sinixt) People.

Sources of the River: Tracking David Thompson across North America, 2nd Edition, by Jack Nisbet (Sasquatch Books, 2007). Recreates the life and times of David Thompson and the fur trade exploration period of the Columbia.

Acknowledgements

With gratitude and honour for the strength of the Sinixt People, living and ancestral, including Patti Bailey, Jim Boyd, Shelly Boyd, Rick Desautel, Mourning Dove, DR Michel, Nancy Michel, Sulustu Moses, Charlie Quintasket, Eva Orr, Virgil Seymour, Robert Watt, LaRae Wiley, Nancy Wynecoop, and Arnold "Judge" Wynecoop.

This story was first performed at the Procter Storytelling Festival in Procter, BC. Thank you, Rick Budd, for asking me to bring the landscape alive. Thanks to Jane Merks and Peter Bartl, who heard the story and first designed and produced a limited edition.

More than a decade later, Tina Wynecoop and Crystal Spicer have offered advice and wisdom to support the story's resurrection. Thank you.

Special gratitude for the creative visions of Leah Best, former director of the Nelson Museum, Archives & Gallery, and the illustrative talent of Nichola Lytle (Pink Dog Designs).

púti? kʷu alá?

We Are Still Here

Eileen Delehanty Pearkes is the author of *The Geography of Memory: Reclaiming the Cultural, Natural, and Spiritual History of the Snayackstx (Sinixt) First People*, *A River Captured: The Columbia River Treaty and Catastrophic Change*, and *The Glass Seed: The Fragile Beauty of Heart, Mind & Memory*. She co-authored, with K. Linda Kivi, *The Inner Green: Exploring Home in the Columbia Mountains*, and has published numerous essays and columns about landscape, imagination, and human history. To learn more about Eileen's work, visit www.edpearkes.com.

Nichola Lytle is a graphic designer and illustrator living in the beautiful mountains of Nelson, BC. She has travelled along the Columbia River out to where the river meets the ocean, exploring her passion for nature, the arts, and Indigenous culture. She teaches illustration and a number of other courses in the digital arts program at Selkirk College. Her work is published with Orca Book Publishers, Thompson Books, and Rubicon, along with several magazines and publications. Awards include the Canadian Toy Council Top 10 Books, Best Bet Award, the Ann Connor Brimer Award, and Best in Business 2014. To learn more about Nichola's work, visit her online at pinkdogdesigns.com.